CW00435638

Rainbows

Lianne Simpson

Copyright © 2020 Lianne Simpson

All rights reserved.

ISBN: 9798615668913

DEDICATION

This book is dedicated to my ever supportive husband who has stood by my side through all the good and the bad.
He has held me up, kept me strong and been my shining light and the end of a very dark tunnel.

My children for bringing so much joy to my life and for just being them.

CONTENTS

RAINBOWS

New opportunities

A great loss

Boxing Day

The void

Changes

New ventures

A rainbow

Moves

Sadness and joy

A new arrival

Memory making

A sad goodbye

A blast from the past

Proud moments

Winner

Battles

Progress

Moving forward

IN THE BEGINNING

The furthest back I can remember was a time of
innocence. Pure joy and elation, from my little
accomplishment.
Clutching my paper bag, concealing my fairy cake.
I had just baked for the first time at nursery and was
eager to show my mother my end product.
I knew she would be proud of me, she always was.

Nursery was my favourite place, my little haven.
Fond memories fill my head of racing to the tricycles,
digging in the sand and splashing in the water tray.
Childhood memories, I hold onto dearly.

My parents appeared happy back then. Or at least
from the perspective of a three year old, they did.

It was my sister and I and Mum and Dad back then.
My baby sister was my pride and joy. Not a soul could

even go near her!

We had a modest home, on the local council housing estate.
Mum kept it nice and Dad worked hard for all the things we had.
The few memories I recall from this time in my life, mostly centered around smells.
I can almost smell them now when I close my eyes.
I remember the smell of the chicken cooking in the oven on a Sunday, the smell of the coal fire and the aroma of cigarette smoke.

We were fortunate to have all the things we could ever want and more.
Plenty of toys to play with, warm beds and a hearty meal every day.
We were blessed.

I remember very fleeting things from that point.

My Nan and my Grandad played a huge part in our lives and often visited several times a week.
I adored them both, but felt closest of all to my Nan.

They were an unmarried couple, but living together as if they were. They once were joined together in matrimony. However this ended many years previous.
Nan would never see my Grandad out on the street and so they cohabited.
To the outside world, they were the perfect, happy couple.
I was oblivious to any issues between them.
They were my happy Nan and Grandad.

I had a close bond with my Uncle, my Mum's
brother.
I looked up to him so. He always had so much time
for me.
Made a fuss of me every time he visited.

We had the most wonderful neighbours and as the
years passed, wonderful friends of my parents.
I affectionately referred to them as my "Aunties" and
"Uncles".
Still to this day, that is what they are.
From a young age I had learned that you didn't have
to be biologically related to someone in order to have
a close bond with them or to view them as family.
These were an extended part of my family and I
cherished them dearly.

I had sparked a good friendship with a young boy
next door, just a year older than myself. We spent
quite a bit of time together. We would play, watch
movies and enjoy each other's company.
He was my earliest memory of a friend.
We shared similar interests and had great fun
together.

My mother had a close friendship with another
couple and from toddler age, I would too play with
their daughter.
I actually have no memories of this, but am told we
were inseparable from that very young age.
She would play a huge part in my life over the years.

In the beginning I had it all. Stability, love, friendships
and fairy cakes.

RAINBOWS

4

CHANGES

The next chapter of my life was about to begin, and I still recall the butterflies in the pit of my stomach.
I remember clinging onto my mums hand tightly as she took me for my first day of Infant School.
I was anxious to begin this new venture and sad to leave my nursery behind.
Some familiar faces followed and I was thankful to have my good friend there with me. She would make things so much easier.
I was sure we could stick together and that brought comfort to me.

I still had issues with bedwetting and so was always worried that others would know, worried others would laugh at me.
Fortunately only my good friend knew my deepest secret and I was sure she would never betray my trust.

Yet that is exactly what she did. Sadly as young children often do. She told others about my bed time secret.
Looking back I know that this was simply the actions of a

young child and no spite was intended. Yet in that moment I was so sad, so cross with her.

Once they knew, it kick started something.
Something I would have to endure for the majority of my school life.
The name calling started at first. Horrendous and vicious names. I was mocked for being a bedwetter, but it didn't stop there.
They often found any new thing, which seemed to be daily, to mock me with.
They moved on from the use of just words and the pushing and shoving started.

I specifically remember a moment on the playground, being pushed to the ground and held there till I forfeited my break time snack.
I lost count of the times the contents of my lunch box was emptied onto the dinner hall floor. How many times they prodded and poked me.

My good friend was still there though although often silent throughout. I guess she secretly feared them too. Feared that if she spoke up, perhaps she would then be a target too.

Her and I spent most days together outside of school. Playing out on the playing areas, playing barbies in the back garden and having a giggle at our weekend sleepovers.
She was my best friend and I couldn't imagine life without her in it.
I wasn't cross with her for revealing my secret.

I used to take solace in the school library, I had the important librarian role. I was even given a shiny orange badge. I was unbelievably proud of that badge. Yet it gave

more cause for the bullies so say unkind things. But I stayed strong. I found comfort in books, took joy from helping the teachers.
I would stack books, clear tables and hide in the corner with my favourite Roald Dahl classic.

I had formed a friendship with a girl in the same class. She had an hearing impairment and she had so much time for me. It was nice to be beside someone that didn't want to tear me down. I then would often spend my breaktime in what was known then as "the deaf unit".
This is where I learned to sign. I was taught how to use basic British Sign Language. It enabled me to communicate more effectively with my friend and became a useful skill that I still know how to use today.

Even through all the difficult times I tried to use tools of distraction to help mask the pain I felt within. The sheer panic I got every day that I entered the school gates. How I wished to not be there. But a great skill that I developed at such a young age was to stand up tall no matter how hard they knocked you down. Keep on smiling, do not show them your fear and better yourself at every given opportunity.

Infant and Junior school was not filled with fond memories but those that would shape my mind and alter my view on humanity and how I dealt with the people around me.

BAD TOUCH

My mother never taught me the things I would need to
know for the situation I found myself in during my days at
infant school.
But then I guess at such a young age, this wasn't deemed
necessary.
I think we were living in a time where ignorance still
surrounded these issues and the education wasn't provided
on such matters.

I was six years old and things were becoming increasingly
harder each day with the bullies and the constant reminder
that I fell far from perfect in their eyes.

During a lesson is when it began and was then repeated
several more times in various locations around the school.

A boy in my class was known by all teachers, mostly for
his negative behavior and was often disciplined for
breaking the rules.
A troubled lad with what I am now informed, had a
difficult home life.

He would take it upon himself to touch me
inappropriately. At the time, in my innocence I never
completely understood what was happening.
I felt uneasy, it made my stomach churn. I knew in my
mind, that what he was doing was not right. I knew that it
wasn't okay.
I built courage to tell him to stop and he ignored my

request and continued to do so. He would find any opportunity in any place he could to do it again.

Looking back, I wish I could have built up the courage to tell my parents, to tell a teacher. Yet the overwhelming fear of it all was just too much. I think I truly believed I too would be in trouble. I was worried my Mum would be cross with me.

I wish I knew then what I understand now.
I wish the education system taught more about the difference between what was a good and bad touch.
Then I wouldn't have had to endure the pain of this alongside the bullies taunts.

I remember laying in my bed and wishing it to stop. I remember praying to a God that I wasn't sure existed. I sat sobbing in my room and for the first time I wished I didn't have to live anymore.
It seemed the only way I could escape the pain and fear I felt daily.
Death would be freedom. Death would be a release.
Perhaps there was a better place to go after you die.

I had so many thoughts like this, so many hopes.
Yet I continued to plod on and continued to put on a brave face.
This became a way of my life.
Being strong was all I knew.

Outside of school, Mum thought it to be a good idea to sign me up to our local Brownies group.
I thoroughly enjoyed the little escape from the norm.
I never experienced any bullying here and the leaders were so lovely.
Unfortunately though it was short lived at this stage.
An unsavory chap had decided to break into the facilities

where the groups was held. He frightened many of the girls, myself included. I am unsure of what his intentions were but the unit decided it was best to put better security on the door.

It was strange attending after that. It never felt the same. Another safe place was ruined for me.

It seemed there were few places to find security, very few times of joy.

I am not sure if you would describe it as depression but I believe I was probably having emotions and symptoms of this by this stage of my life.

By the end of year six, I had endured six years of torment. I was ready for it to be over.

My final memory of this school, was sitting on the playground, clutching my little notepad. Hoping someone would want to sign mine. Hoping someone cared to say goodbye. Not a single person did. The only note within that pad, was one from my Nan and from my Mum.

It became the norm to me. I had adapted and unfortunately had a fairly negative outlook on life. I had my guard firmly up and assumed the worst in all. This would be my new coping mechanism. My new strategy for dealing with life.

A MAZE

Memories come flooding back, of standing and feeling completely overwhelmed.
Staring up at these huge buildings and suddenly feeling so small.
Those were my first thoughts upon beginning secondary school.
I had no optimism and was under no illusion. I never once believed that this next phase in my life would be any different from the last.

Mum had already arranged for measures to be put in place, during a meeting she had held right before the summer.
What more could an 11 year old want, than a brightly coloured red card to excuse herself from the class to go to the toilet.
That was now in my possession, my get out card.
Little did I know at that stage, just how useful that would prove.

You see I had experienced many a kidney infection and was still battling my ongoing night time wetting.
I was very aware now though of the importance of self-

care.

I was determined to ensure I gave them no cause to bully me. No reason to highlight my differences.

My only hope, was that over the summer holidays, people had forgotten the names that used to call me. Hoped they had forgotten my embarrassing night time issue.

I couldn't have been more wrong.

I cannot not remember exactly how long it was before it started again, but from recollection it couldn't have been that far into the school year.

I am mostly basing this on my lack of familiarity with the school still at this point.

I would still find myself getting lost in what felt like a maze of buildings and classrooms.

I often found myself in the wrong place and then became somewhat of a laughing stock when I arrived late to my lessons.

I guess my anxiety played a huge part in all of this. I just seemed to panic all too easily.

My best friend had followed me to the same school and this bought me a great deal of comfort.

Although for the majority of the school day, I would not see her and our arrangement of friendship used to mainly be that we would meet after the school day.

It didn't help of course that my form room was completely different to the few people I actually spoke to.

The only people that gave me time of day were in a completely different classroom to me.

I did however strike up two new friendships.

Two other girls whom I feel could relate to my issues.

Both themselves at one point or another, being at the receiving end of a bully.

Both personalities not dissimilar from my own.

Both shy and fairly withdrawn characters.
But a good lifetime friendship had begun with them both.

They were my saving grace and my comfort. When days were dark and things became unbearable, it was nice to have that someone to confide in. That someone that understood the feelings I was experiencing.

The first year was a bit of a blur.
With only the occasional thing remaining etched in my mind.
I think when you have experienced hard times. When you have developed an negative outlook on life, it is then really difficult to reflect on the positive memories within your mind.

Bullying was on a whole other level in secondary school.
I wasn't sure it could actually be any worse from what I had already had to endure.
But the language became more colourful, the insults more personal and the attacks were more vicious.

I think my Mum could safely say, she lost count of the occasions that she would have to visit the school. Meetings to have with the senior members of staff.
Trying relentlessly to put a stop to the things I had to go through on a regular basis.

I look back during this time and look for reasons. My mind tells me that perhaps these characters had distressing home lives. Perhaps they were low in their own self esteem.
I'm not sure.
I truly believe that some were just unpleasant people and that wouldn't change even into their adult lives.

CONFLICTS

After surviving my first year of secondary school.
I was ready for a break.
Ready for some release and time away from the daily
panics and upsets.

The summer holidays were always a great time for me.
I enjoyed spending time with my friends without fear of
being judged.
I enjoyed being able to let go just that little bit more and I
could almost forget what was awaiting me when I
returned.

Home life at this point though had begun to change.
Mum and Dad had already had my newest little sister.
But the difficulties in their relationship seemed to become
more obvious.
They would argue almost every day.
Mum was definitely the more vocal of the two.
Her shouts could be heard from the bottom of our street.
I think though, looking back. It was obvious that a great
deal of my Mums frustrations and anger were mostly
linked to her distressing childhood.

It was around these time I remember being enlightened on the things my mum had to witness on a daily basis as a child.
My perfectly happy Nan and Grandad had been the root cause of her character and how she then handled difficult situations.
It came to light that my Grandad was a raging alcoholic through her youth and much into her young adulthood too.
This, however used to alter the person he was.
He was very abusive towards my Nan and was not shy about doing so when my Mum and Uncle were present.
He would often have my Nan is a hospitalised state, a quivering mess on the floor or in such states that no child should have to see.

From what I have been told, my Mum was her little sidekick through the tough times. She was often the one picking her up. Standing up to my Grandad through his angry bouts.
She was my inspiration. Such a true warrior.
Yet my Uncle couldn't have been any more different.
He seemed the weaker of the two. Often abandoning her and leaving her to face the aftermath of Grandads angry outbursts, alone.
He couldn't cope with it I guess. His character appeared to have been far weaker than my Mum's.

Having said all of this. My Mum was also the most loving and supportive person I had ever known. She was my knight in most situations. She would do all she could to protect me. She wouldn't stand for the things I went through at school. She fought my every battle alongside me all the time.

I was never sure what caused the arguments between my parents, but I would avoid being at home where possible.

At this point I wasn't sure where I preferred to be.
My best friend and I would usually entertain ourselves
during the school holidays.
Exploring places around the town we lived. Often finding
ourselves getting up to mischief. But no different from
most others of our age.

I can still recall my Mums face as I presented her with my
tar soaked shoes on our doorstep.
Our bridge building skills left a lot to be desired and I had
fallen into a tar pit.
Mum wasn't too impressed with my newly dyed footwear.

We never caused any harm to others. We were respectful
of others property.
But those were some of the greatest times I had.
The last time I remember feeling so free, so able to enjoy
being a child.
For those moments were the last time I truly felt that way.

My bedroom at that time was also my little escape.
I would often be found hiding there to avoid the conflicts
between my parents.
This was the time in my life when my OCD had started.

I never realised at the time. It is only over years gone by
that I realised how far back it had begun.
I used my tidiness and want for perfection as a distraction.
Everything had its place, everything was uniformed and
organised in such a way.
I even kept lists to ensure things remained the same.
Tidying and cleaning my room was a good distraction. An
effective coping mechanism that I would depend on
throughout my life.

RAINBOWS

RELEASE

I hadn't quite realised how tough this next year was going
to be.
Over the course of the summer, everyone had changed.
New attitudes had formed. Some more negatively than
others.
They didn't wait long. Once we had settled into our new
school year, the taunting and attacks begun again.

My body was developing and I remember feelings of
confusion around this time.
Unsure of how to handle these changes and the emotions I
felt within.
I guess developing into a teenager was the cause.

I feared every day now, awoke in the mornings with pains
of anxiety and despair in my body.
The bedwetting only increased with my low mood.
I could see no end in sight for that.
I was always too embarrassed to invite friends for
sleepovers, in case they knew.
Other than my best friend of course. She never judged me.

RAINBOWS

I was comfortable with her.

But back then we had what could only be described, as
plastic carrier bag like material on my mattress and pillows.
It was both irritating and unbelievably uncomfortable.
I could never allow others to see these or know that I had
to use them.

I remember feeling excited when my Mum first allowed
me to have money to spend in the cafeteria at school.
I felt so grown up being able to buy my own lunch.
At least they couldn't steal my packed lunch any more.
No, they stole my money instead.
On more occasions than I care to remember, my lunch
money was stolen.
I was so worried to tell my Mum and so I remained silent
on the matter.
I went hungry for the majority of the week.

I now spent most of my break times at school, hiding and
attempting to blend into the background.
It didn't always work.
The bullying spilled into the classrooms too. With teachers
oblivious or perhaps they just avoided the confrontation.
I spent a lot of lessons with someone's foot firmly placed
on the back of my chair. Kicking out at me till I cried.

I had bruises from their kicks in the playground, rips in my
clothes and I felt as if I was never going to be good
enough for anyone.

They damaged my self-esteem so much, any worth I had
left inside had diminished.

This was the first time I remember inflicting harm onto
myself.
I began, through frustration, pinching myself.

I would get so distressed and upset, this felt like a release from that.

The pinching led to extreme scratching.

I would scratch my skin till it burned, till I brought blood to the surface. It was only at that point did I feel a release for the tensions building within my body.

A compass became a handy tool and I would regularly jab it into my thighs.

Self-harming became my new release. This was something I sought to do each day. It was the only way I could get through a day. The only way I could keep my mind focused.

The only trouble is though, I didn't want to stop there.

I wanted to die.

Each night I would lay in my bed and think of ways that I could do it.

I was so tired of the pain in my head. So worn from the aching in my heart.

I wasn't good enough anyway, so nobody would miss me if I wasn't there.

I was just a huge inconvenience to most.

The ugly duckling.

I was fed up with being their pin cushion, fed up with being their target.

On one very desperate and sad day, I tried to do just that.

Something stopped me. Thoughts of my parents, my sisters.

How they would feel without me.

I couldn't hurt them. This wasn't their fault.

It took a huge amount of restraint to not continue with what I was doing.

But I couldn't allow my Mum to find me in that way.

I was fed up though, and I couldn't comprehend how I would survive another day at their hands.

RAINBOWS

HABITS

Tucked behind a small grass hill at one of our local park,
myself and my best friend sat giggling.
We were proud of ourselves for sneaking out one of her
Dads pre-rolled cigarettes.
We were intrigued by its greenish outer colour and curious
to how it may taste.
Between us, after several attempts, successfully lit the
rolled cigarette.
Needless to say it wasn't what we were expecting. We
coughed and spluttered and tossed it away.
I would love to say we learned a lesson and never did it
again, but sadly that was not the case.

We continued to sneak out tobacco and cigarettes.
Smoking became our naughty little habit that we would
frequently sneak off to do.
It was quickly something I went to for comfort during
really difficult times.

Looking back, I wonder if my parents actually noticed. I
mean the smell of cigarettes is really not concealable. I
must have used ridiculous amounts of body spray and

practically had shares in Wrigglys chewing gum. By some miracle they never detected it, or perhaps were just ignorant to it and didn't want to acknowledge it.

It never seemed quite enough though and my smoking habit was soon accompanied but another unhealthy one.

Myself and my best friend amongst a few other characters that we had befriended outside of school, would frequently attempt to get members of the public to purchase us alcohol from the local shops.
We would regularly indulge in a bottle of cheap cider and popular alcopops.
We usually situated ourselves in discreet places and did this most weekends.
We snuck home intoxicated on more times than I care to remember.
Something else I am shocked remained unnoticed by my parents.
Our habit only grew and we consumed more and more alcohol as time went on.

We never caused any trouble and kept ourselves away from others as best we could. We were never offensive and always respectful of our surroundings.
Just teenagers caught up in a world of alcohol and cigarettes.
Being raised in homes where alcohol was drank freely, particularly at weekends and having parents that had smoking habits, perhaps it was inevitable we too would be tempted.

I began to notice my friends showing interests towards the opposite sex. Talking of crushes on others that we went to school with. I felt a little different, felt odd.
I never yet had those thoughts or feelings.
I was content living in my own bubble. My escape from

the torture I faced daily.

I guess I always assumed that others just looked at me with disgust and nobody could possibly ever look at me any differently.

I spent most days being ridiculed for my looks so why would anyone think any different.

I listened to my friends tales of sneaky kisses with boys. Of their juvenile relationships and entertaining spin the bottle stories.

I had my first 'grown up' party invitation. I was anything but excited though. The girl that had invited me took pity on me I felt.

She had invited quite a large portion of our year group too. I couldn't think of anything worse.

Mum encouraged me to attend. Said it would "do me good".

I reluctantly went along. I had never felt more out of my depth.

I settled into the evening of music and food. It wasn't as bad as I had anticipated.

That was before they cracked out the spin the bottle game.

That dreaded game that I giggled about when my friends told of their experiences.

As I sat in a circles of girls and boys, I tensed my body and crossed my fingers.

I was praying secretly that the bottle wouldn't point towards me.

Unfortunately my fear was realised.

I sunk in despair as I awaited the mocking.

The young lad just giggled and refused to "go near that".

I sunk a little further.

I slipped out of the room, grabbed my coat and left.

I took a lonely and sad walk home. I would never attend one of these again.

RAINBOWS

INNOCENCE

She was giddy with excitement when she told me of her little secret.
My best friend had just confided in me, that she was seeing an older boy.
She had been sneaking out in order to meet up with him.
There was no doubting that if her parents were aware than she would have been in some serious trouble.

I think naivety played a huge part in how we dealt with every situation then.
I actually remember thinking how unbelievably 'cool' it was. Jealous even.
I think once more, the lack of understanding around life's dangers and risk avoidance was a huge factor in our poor decision making.

I kept her little secret and continued to admire her as she continued her relationship in secret. I wish I had the awareness then to advise her correctly, to deter her from making these poor choices.

Still heavily drinking, we attended a party being held for

her younger sister.
All of the adults in attendance were drinking. So accessing
alcohol wasn't much of a challenge.
She had previously mentioned that her secret love interest
had a friend that was interested to meet with me.
In that moment I had agreed to do just that.
I think some part of me, knew that I was making a bad
choice.
Yet so desperate for some positive attention and for
someone to actually show an interest in me, I went along
with it.

So on that night, we slipped away.
We had arranged to be collected in their car.
I had a knot in the pit of my stomach the entire time.
But above all that I was excited to go along for the ride.
I felt like for once, I was being respected. I was wanted.

As we drove further away, I whispered to my friend and
questioned where we were going. She didn't seem to know.
It soon became clear and we pulled up in a secluded area.
There was zero lighting and this particular area was
surrounded by trees.
I think that was the first time I felt regret.
In that instance I knew we shouldn't be there, I did not
feel safe.

The love interest and my friend left the vehicle. I watched
as there shadowy figures disappeared off in the
overgrowth.
A cold sensation ran through my body. I was feeling afraid.
I wanted to run. I knew I was stuck.

He never really said much and most of the things he did
utter actually appear like a mist in my mind now.
I could barely recognise the words being spoken.

He had joined me in the back.
I then knew exactly what his intentions were and with
nowhere to run, I knew I had no choice.

I can still feel my tear soaked cheeks.
I uttered quiet words but I clearly indicated I did not want
to participate.
He continued anyway.

He treated me like a piece of meat. It felt as if he was
tearing my body in half.
I ached all over, I could struggle no more.
I allowed him to rob me of my innocence whilst my tears
streamed down my face, the stench of his aftershave stuck
up my nostrils and the touch of his skin made mine
terribly crawl.

He discarded me in the same manner in which he had
treated me.
I could see the blood soaked seats beneath me.

They both returned to the car.
It was an unbelievably quiet journey back.
My legs were so sore, my tights were ripped.
The only active thought in my mind was how potentially
cross my Mum would be if she see how badly torn my
tights were.

It was a blur after that. I never realised just how different I
would feel after that. I never truly understood the true
implications on my mental health and how much it had
altered my outlook on my future.

The night remained a secret between us. I could not and
did not ever want a soul knowing.
I was judged enough. I blamed myself and that's how I
spent many long years after.

RAINBOWS

RETALIATION

I think my perception on life had certainly been altered. I had undeniable trust issues and my attitude towards people in general had changed.

My personality developed and I no longer wanted to be the pushover I was always perceived to be.

It all began with a day at school.
Nothing unusual, a group of girls followed me around the school grounds during break time. Shouting abusive words, pushing me beyond my limits. Laughing at me as they could see the anger building within me.

It almost felt as if they had hit a switch and deep within me a terrible anger stirred. My body seemed to move quicker than my brain could compute.
I lashed out and with one strong punch, I sent her tumbling to the ground.
I felt a sudden release and a great weight lift from my shoulders.
I felt no regret, I wasn't even sorry.
I walked on and proceeded with my day as normal.

RAINBOWS

My Mum was of course called into the school to discuss
the incident and I was issued with a letter of suspension.
My Mum then went on to appeal the decision to remove
me short term from school.

Much to my dismay, she won the argument.
They lifted the ban and agreed it was an isolated incident
and completely out of character.

Needless to say, the bullies retreated. I could finish my
remaining years without fear of being attacked.
I had the occasional word thrown in my direction, but
generally they kept a wide birth.

My character was not the same. I became quite hard faced.
I had my guard firmly up and no one was getting in.

I had started a new phase in my life. A desire to be
different. To find the person I really wanted to be.
I had a multitude of piercings and altered the colour of my
hair. I was trying to re-invent myself.
I think by the time I had finished school, I had probably
had all the colours of the rainbow upon my head.

With my every growing cigarette and drinking habit, I
needed the funds to keep purchasing the items.

I took to shop theft. I stole an array of things. From pens,
to yoyo's, to make up and sweets.
This is not one of my proudest life choices but in those
moments I would have risked most things in order to keep
fueling my addiction.

I would go on to sell the items to my school peers.
Eventually people would put in requests for things for me
to take.

It was a vicious cycle to be in and one I eventually did
break free from.

My Mum was happy to buy me alcohol in moderation as
long as I drank it in the safety of my home.
Unbeknown to her, this was not always the case.

I spent many more days out of the house, to avoid the
arguments between my parents.
So much frequent shouting and harsh words being used.
I couldn't handle it in all honesty.

I spent many an evening out with friends, wondering the
streets. Sipping cider and smoking. Occasionaly heading to
each other's houses.

I did a little work in an salon with a friend of the family. It
didn't pay brilliantly but it gave me a little time away from
the thoughts distracting my mind.
I lived very briefly with my Uncle and I think it helped
bring clarity to things.

Once again I was back home and I managed to secure a
little job as a waitress in a local burger joint. I loved my
new found independence and was pleased to have my own
little income.
It kept me level headed too and gave me better focus.
I made new friends and gained a new found confidence.

I remained here for some time before moving on to a new
waitressing role in my Aunties pub.
All little jobs around this stage of my life never lasted too
long but I enjoyed learning new skills and had a knack for
blending into my surroundings.

Soon I would be sixteen and I would finally be free from
the school chains.

RAINBOWS

END OF A PHASE

I could almost smell the freedom from the chains I had
been tied up in for the past five years.
Soon enough I would be able to leave all of this behind
me.
After all these months of little or no teasing from them,
they had decided to set their focus on me once more,
during our exams.
For the majority of my end of school exams, I had to
endure the familiar kicking sensation against the back of
my chair.
I struggled to keep my mind focused whilst they
continually took pleasure in bringing me discomfort.

On one particular occasion, I alerted a teacher to the
incident.
I was reminded to 'just get on with it' and left to tolerate
the persistent foot.
Needless to say I was not sorry when the final page closed
on my last exam.
They could harm me no more.

I can still remember the excited questions from friends

about whether I was planning on attending sixth form. I could not bear the thought of returning to the place that had given me so many terrible memories.
I was pleased to be leaving that where it belonged, in the past.

My best friend was having a tough time with things around this stage.
She struggled to attend for the majority of our final school year.
This was mostly down to her Dad passing away.
It was such a sad thing to see her go through, I had never seen her quite so low.
We were all so very fond of him and he played a huge part in all of our lives.
He was a well-respected and loved man. He never took life all too seriously and bought so much joy and laughter to all he came across.
I supported her through the times that followed, helped lift her when she didn't feel like standing.
Together with my Mum we showed a great deal of support and comfort to the whole family as a unit.
I know she truly appreciated having me by her side.

With the holidays upon us, I was filled with joy and all the things I could fill my time with.
It was at this point that I took on the role of a Junior Hair Stylist, in a popular salon in town.
It was an exciting opportunity and finally something I could see myself doing.
For the first time in a long while, I could see a future.

Between working and having the typical teenage fun with my friends, my parents announced their separation.
It was a long time coming but even so, it was hard to see my Mum cry so much.
My youngest sister took it the hardest and struggled to

adjust to things.

My other sister and I stood firmly by Mums side and helped keep her strong through a difficult time.

Seeing Dad leave was heartbreaking.

Through all the bad times, the shouting and the upset. We were saying goodbye to all the joy, because it certainly did outweigh the bad.

Mum seemed to plod on and took to enjoying more time with friends. It was nice to see her let go.

She informed me that I could hold a party at our home. A school leavers party, to celebrate the exam results we had all just received.

I was over the moon with this idea.

I immediately started to invite friends and plan how the party would go.

Mum purchased alcohol for us all. I had the best Mum in the world.

I wondered how many other parents would be 'cool' enough to do this.

I felt excited and it was nice to finally have a crowd of people that wanted to spend time with me.

In the days leading up to the party, we had arranged a few social gatherings with my best friend, her mother and new partner.

During the holidays I had inadvertently begun a relationship with his son.

He was two years younger than I and known for being quite the trouble maker.

It was nice to have a little interest though and so I continued the pointless relationship.

He was quite aggressive towards me, he would speak down to me and often 'playfully' hit me on the arm.

An occasion in a pub though, see my Mum and his Dad see the kind of person he truly was when he publicly hit me 'affectionately' and he then had to deal with the wrath

RAINBOWS

of my Mum.

THE PARTY

Party night was finally here. I had filled the kitchen with a vast selection of alcohol and stacked my CD collection on the breakfast bar.
The music was playing already and my Mum was readying herself for a night out with friends.
She wasn't going far and she planned to allow me some time with my friends.
As people started to arrive I felt excited and quite grown up actually, for holding this party.

I did however have a shift at the salon the following day, so I knew I could not go too crazy but intended to enjoy the evening anyway.

There were people from my previous place of work, a handful of school friends, my best friend and a few others that actually remain to be blurred figures in my mind.

The evening progressed and I had only had just the two drinks. I remember feeling particularly tired. I didn't feel drunk, that was a sensation I had felt on many occasions before.

RAINBOWS

I felt as if I needed to sleep.

I took myself away for a little lay down in my bed.
The room was spinning and I couldn't seem to focus very
well at all.
I lay there and felt my eyelids becoming heavy although
they remained open.
I heard the creak of my door opening and two figures
appeared.
One was a male that I had befriended via my best friend
and the other was my now ex-boyfriend.
After the night in the pub, I had put an end to our
relationship.
I was not going to be anyone's punch bag.

Music began to play on my stereo, I'm not too sure who
put it on.
I can still hear the songs playing on loop through my mind
now.
They were quite argumentative as they moved themselves
around my room.
Quite an odd pairing of people to be together and an very
unlikely friendship.
I was confused as to what they were both doing in my
room.

The music from downstairs vibrated through the ceiling
and I wondered if anyone had even noticed the three of us
were missing.

I felt uneasy as they both plonked themselves on my bed.
It wasn't long before their intentions became apparent.

I asked them to leave through mumbled breath yet they
remained.
Then what followed was nothing short of one of the
hardest things I have ever had to endure.

39

The forcefulness in their bodies bought horrific memories back to mind and the fear that I had felt previously, had returned.
I was frozen, I felt as if my brain was telling my body to move yet it remained almost lifeless on the bed.
The Scream in my throat almost seemed stuck and I could feel a familiar sensation on my cheeks as the tears rolled down.

They pulled me about and took turns to use me in whichever way they deemed fit.
I recall an argument between the pair on 'who's turn it was next'.
They treated me like a fairground ride, like I wasn't a human life, deserving of any kind of respect.

I cannot forget the undeniable burning sensation on my chest as the ash from one of their cigarettes dropped onto me.
Burning me and leaving marks that would later be examined.
I told them to stop and leave once more and yet they ignored my requests and brushed aside my pleas.
I felt an immense sensation of panic and prayed that someone would realise and help me.

I'm not sure how long this torment went on for and understandably there are parts which still remain quite unfocused in my mind.
But the shrill scream from my sister still echoes through my ears.
She had discovered the scene and from what I was later told, ran to get help.

My mum had already returned from her evening out and was downstairs enjoying a chat with some friends, and the party seemed to carry on around her.

As I now understand some had already left though and returned to their homes.

I remember lots of screaming after that, shouts and a series of bangs and loud noises.

I remained in an awful state upon my bed, familiar blood stains surrounded me and that familiar feeling in the pit of my stomach was there.
Was this really happening again?

The night became somewhat of a blur after that.
I could never forget the look in my sisters face, the sheer panic in her eyes.
The screams from my Mum, the crashing sound of furniture being thrown.
All whilst I remained in a state of shock and disbelief upon my bed.

The music still played on my stereo and yet the night seemed now awfully quiet.

I couldn't cry anymore, instead I felt as if my body was shutting down.
Retreating to an hedgehog like state.

I fleetingly remember different figures appearing in my room, words of comfort and reassurance filled the air. But I remained in a shell shocked like state and I am not even sure I responded to any of them.

The police were called and the terror behind me was not yet over.
For the moments that followed would be some of the most difficult and challenging things I would ever have to deal with.

At this moment I did not feel as if I had the strength nor the courage to fight this. I felt weaker than ever.

CRIME SCENE

The days that followed that dreaded night were some of
the hardest yet.
I had to undergo a series of invasive tests and questions.
I must have retold the event a dozen times already.
I had tests that involved me having to bare my body to
which I found incredibly difficult given the nature of
things I had just experienced.
Every mark on my body was photographed and every tiny
piece of forensic evidence was collected.

My house resembled a crime scene, it all felt rather surreal
at the time. I hid away from most of it all.
My Mum handled things and kept everyone going.

I turned to drink more than ever. I had given up my job at
the salon, I couldn't even face the outside world.
I lay in bed most days, smoking one packet of cigarettes
after another.
It never filled the empty space within me though, it never

erased the thoughts racing through my mind.

A doctor was contacted and I was prescribed the first ever anti-depressants I would take.
I detested how they made me feel. I was reassured that they would get better and my body would adjust but they never got any easier to take.
They caused me to have more of a disturbed night's sleep and constantly left me feeling drowsy.
I stopped taking them.

After weeks of examining, testing, questioning and explorative work, we were issued with a date of when the case would be taken to court.

Shortly after, articles appeared in newspapers, word spread around the neighbourhood.
Such awful things were spoken of me in the newspapers.
Such terrible gossip circled the streets.

I tried to bury my head, tried to move on with my life.
Kept myself going, put on a brave face.
The truth was I was crumbling within.

Soon enough being at home was just too much for all involved. I believe that my family were having a hard time adjusting to my mood swings, to my low mood and stress.

I moved in with my Nan and Grandad.

My Mum, however, managed to convince the school to have me back to attend sixth form.
I joined three months into the year so had missed quite a bit.
They were aware of my situation and were very accommodating.
I kept my head down and used my determination and

strong will to complete my course.

I built a new friendship group and became closer than ever to my good friend. She became a rock to me. My go to for talking and opening up.
My best friend and I drifted apart and didn't speak during this point in my life.
Thank goodness for my wonderful good friend, I'm not sure I could have survived without her relentless support.

She and I shared the same course and we often helped each other throughout.
We spent time together outside of school too and were inseparable a lot of the time.

During this time I began receiving a barrage of abuse.
Threatening letters posted through my door, a glass bottle tossed at my head, attacked and abuse hurled at me in the streets.
Family and friends of my attackers were determined to make my life as miserable as possible. As if I hadn't been through enough.

Through all of these hard times my good friend stayed strong for me, my Mum supported and of course my Nan.

The case eventually made it to a court room.
My Mum and Dad both attended for support.
Fortunately I did not have to appear inside the court room and could give my statement via a video link.
I had great support from the lady heading my case and I could not have been more thankful for the work of the police force.

The defense team ripped me apart and every word I uttered.
They won.

RAINBOWS

Through insufficient evidence and a case of one word
against another, they walked away.
They tore my life apart and now they were free to go.

MOVING ON

I spent the next year living with my Grandparents, I passed
my sixth form course with flying colours and had even
secured a job at the cinema. I started on the same day as
friend I had made during my sixth form days and a new
face.

I loved my new role and I made a fantastic new group of
friends.
It gave me a new sense of worth, something I had craved
for such a long time.
I felt as if some form of normality was finally resumed.

I spent the majority of my time working, it helped to
occupy my mind.
In my free time I would head out with friends. We drank
most weekends and with what free time we had.
Spending time in nightclubs, pubs and house parties.
Nothing unusual for a bunch of eighteen year old's.

My Nan was wonderful throughout. She cooked me

delicious home cooked meals, allowed me the freedom to come and go as I pleased and only asked for a small amount of money towards my living.
She was just what I needed during this time of my life.

Eventually though I needed to move on, needed my own space.
After much searching and the help of a friend, I was able to secure a privately rented house. I shared the accommodation with a work colleague so we could split the responsibility of rent, shopping and bills.
It was the ideal arrangement.

I continued to pursue a career in the cinema industry and secured myself the role of supervisor, I was unbelievably proud of myself.
I had only been there a little under three months so it was a huge accomplishment.
I then had a responsibility of supervising a team of staff.
I put together rotas, floorplans, did stock taking, orders and more.
I felt important, needed and respected. It was a nice feeling.

Outside of work remained pretty much the same, I had several house parties and gatherings in my new house.
I was always responsible though and rent and bills always came first.
However my house mate had lost his job and was struggling to hold down permanent employment so I soon became the sole bill payer in the property.

This was tough on a cinema wage and eventually he moved out.
I struggled to make ends meet and often went hungry.
My Mum was often my savior during these dark times and would frequently deliver parcels of food to me.

RAINBOWS

But there were many times where I hid from her the lack of money for food I had.

My diet mostly consisted of plain pasta and cheap pizzas.

A friend of mine had introduced me to Cannabis one day.
I had a history of leg pains and it was quickly becoming obvious that it was not the growing pains that my doctors spent years telling my Mum it was.
It seemed, I was in fact struggling with Arthritis.
These pains would floor me and often see me curled in a ball of sheer agony.
Cannabis proved to be a relief to this pain and quickly became something I turned to on a regular basis.
I lessened the amount of alcohol I was consuming and smoked this instead in replacement of it.
It was a great help for many reasons and I admittedly was dependent on it for quite some years.

One particular night, see me sat alone and quietly watching television. An unexpected knock came at the door.
It was my Dad, carrying a black sack over his shoulder and a case in the other hand.
He had been kicked out from his lodgings and was seeking a place to stay.
Since I had a spare room, I allowed him to stay and took him in from the cold.

My Dad stayed with me for a few months, just till he managed to find his feet again. I didn't mind helping him and actually welcomed the company and extra income.
It was actually a small blessing in times of financial hardship.

Unfortunately though, I was then served notice to leave my home. The house hunting began again.

49

OLD FACES

My Mum had not long had my baby brother and was
adjusting to life as an older parent.
She had a new partner and seemed happy.
It was nice to see her smile after so many years of being
unhappy.
My dad had eventually moved back into his lodgings and
was in a relationship with an older woman.
Life seemed to just slowly move forward.

It wasn't long before I left my position at the cinema and
took on two new jobs.
I managed to get myself a job at the new nightclub in town
and picked up a little part time cleaning position at the
local council.
It was ideal and both together bought in a generous
income.

The nightclub was somewhat out of my comfort zone and
a new thing for me to learn but I thoroughly enjoyed it.
My confidence was growing daily and my ability to be in
crowds had improved.
I would often be tested by difficult customers and

challenging situations. It helped to build on my ever growing strong personality and I was pleased with the person I was becoming.

I am still unsure at how it happened but my best friend had returned to my life.
We seemed to draw a line under days gone by and put rest to all the years and reasons behind us not speaking with one another.
It was odd, because it was as if we had never been apart.
We began spending time together again, although not as frequently as we once did.
I was happy to have her back in my life, I had missed her terribly.

It wasn't long before she announced her pregnancy to me.
I was over the moon for her.
I truly believed she would be a wonderful Mother.

It wasn't much of wait till I discovered I too was pregnant.
We both carried our first child together.
It was nice to share the journey alongside her. We shared our fears and worries and helped each other adjust to our news.
It was not uncommon for us to share important life changes and things together. We always seemed connected in that way.

The months ahead seem to fly by and she then gave birth to a healthy baby boy, ten days later I gave birth to a healthy baby girl.

We were new Mums together and I couldn't have been happier or more grateful to have her sharing the journey alongside me.

SURPRISES

I took to motherhood far easier than I ever expected.
I adored my baby girl and everything I did was all for her.
I could spend hours just watching her sleep.
I doted on her and so did everyone else.

My Mum, my Nan and even my Dad were thrilled to meet
the newest addition to our family.

I beamed with pride, every time I got to take her out. She
was mine and I loved her unconditionally and the best
thing was, she loved me too.

I watched her develop into a confident little toddler.
She crawled and walked quicker than expected and was
learning new words every day.
She utterly amazed me with all she could do.

I was healthy enough in general until I started to develop
pains in my stomach.
After a visit to the doctors, I was referred for a scan.
During the scan I was informed by the sonographer that
the cause was Polycystic Ovary Syndrome (PCOS).
After a chat with my doctor and a breakdown of what this

meant. I was informed that this would mean my fertility would now be affected.
I was told that I needed to prepare myself and understand I would most likely have no more children.

It was quite a hard bit of news to swallow. Even though I had this beautiful little girl whom I adored. I couldn't help but feel utter sadness about not being able to give her a brother or a sister.

I managed to push it to the back of my mind and carried on as normal.

I started to feel quite poorly one day and looking in the mirror had noticed I had put on a significant amount of weight.
If I was honest right then, I hadn't been feeling myself for quite some weeks.

I decided to book a doctors appointment.

When I arrived, I was sure he was going to tell me that it was all in fact just symptoms of my newly diagnosed condition.
He insisted on carrying out a pregnancy test, even after me assuring him this was an impossibility.
I obliged anyway.

I stood and proceeded to put my coat on ready to leave.
The doctor then surprisingly told me to take a seat. As I did, he dropped the news that I was in fact expecting another baby.
This was a huge shock after finally adjusting to the idea of never having another.

He examined me and guessed I was already at the very least three months pregnant.

I left, my head in a bit of a spin.
Walking home, I could think of nothing but the news I
had just been delivered.

I had to await a scan to date my pregnancy, to see if all was
progressing okay.

I couldn't quite accept it and managed to convince myself
that he had got it very wrong.

A few days later, a letter dropped onto my door mat.
It was of course the date for my scan.
I still failed to see how this was even a possibility.
I was sadly in a state of denial.

I lay patiently upon the sonographers bed whilst she
squirted the cold gel on my stomach.
As she began to scan me, she turned the screen so I could
see.
Sure enough there he was. My baby boy, that I hadn't even
realised was there.
It transpired that I was a lot further along than they had
estimated too. Just under five months.

It was a lot of information to digest and I remained quite
shocked for some time.
During my scan I was told I had a condition called
Placenta Previa. Basically my placenta covered my cervix.
If this remained there till the end of my pregnancy, I
would then not be able to deliver my baby without surgery.

I was monitored closely throughout before they decided to
arrange for me to have a cesarean section.

I became very depressed and was diagnosed with Anti-
Natal Depression.

BLUE LIGHTS

The next two months seemed to fly by and I was still struggling with the acceptance of my pregnancy and still not able to come to terms with it all.

I had a routine consultation appointment to discuss the birth plan. Discuss how the procedure would work and what I needed to expect.

I listened and took on board all the information and left for the journey home.
It was a good hour walk home from the hospital but one that took that little bit longer with all the additional weight I was now carrying.

Half way into my journey back, I developed a painful stitch-like feeling in my side.
Walking was incredibly painful and the journey back became quite unbearable.
Once home, I proceeded to continue with my jobs as normal and still the pain did not shift.
After a little while, the pains had spread to my back. It quickly became obvious that I was in labour.

55

I was only eight months pregnant and the words of the
consultant rang through my head.
I could not deliver this baby in the natural manner or we
could both die.
Panic spread through my body and immediately I
telephoned my midwife, whom didn't hesitate to telephone
for an ambulance.

After a small debate with the paramedics whom seemed
very prepared to deliver my baby within my flat and a firm
talking to from my midwife, they eventually had me loaded
in the back of the ambulance.

My contractions quickened at an alarming rate and the
ambulance sped along, siren blaring.
I remember in my drowsy state, complaining that they felt
it paramount to use the flashing blue lights.
They giggled and kept me calm through the very quick and
scary journey.

We arrived at the hospital in no time at all and as quick as
anything, I was hooked up to machines and had a team of
faces surrounding my bed.
They monitored me for a short time and kept checking for
signs of dilation.
The painful contractions continued and I was at that point
loaded up with pain relief.

I remember crying and blaming myself. I always pushed
myself too far. I was sure I was the cause.

In a whirlwind of events, I was whisked into theatre.
After lots of pulling, tugging and panic from me. He was
finally here.
He was very quiet though and I awaited his little baby cry.
I recalled my first born being very vocal indeed.
He needed a little support getting his lungs kick started

and in no time at all, he was making his presence known.

He was tiny in comparison to my first, to be expected with
his premature arrival.
He was checked over and given the all clear to accompany
me to the ward.

Over the next 24 hours, I became incredibly impatient and
frustrated. Not being able to move my legs was hard when
you had a dependent newborn right beside you. I missed
my baby girl back home and spent most hours crying to be
home.
I watched him closely though over the day and he didn't
appear right to me at all.
His lips appeared a tinge of blue in colour. I alerted the
medical staff and was reassured that he was absolutely fine.
The day went on and I wasn't satisfied that he was actually
okay and became concerned with his shallow breathing.

I asked for a doctor, and he arrived fairly promptly.
Upon inspection, he was then moved to the Special Care
Baby Unit. He was in fact having difficulty with his
breathing and that was causing the blueish colouring on his
lips.
I suddenly felt incredibly alone.

Unable to move, I sat sobbing on my bed as I watched the
other new Mum's cradle their babies.

I was already experiencing great pain from my mental
health and now they had taken my baby away.

In those moments away from him, I had somehow
managed to convince myself that I wouldn't be taking my
baby home. I had convinced myself he had died.

CONTROL

As I sat gazing at the empty cot at my bedside, I couldn't help but blame myself.
I felt a deep void within, he wasn't here where he was supposed to be.

I visited the hospital regularly during his stay there. I sat beside him and encouraged him to get better enough and strong enough to be able to go home.
Yet I had managed to convince myself that he did not belong to me.

I still remember the shock in the eyes of the midwives and nurses as I told them they had given me the wrong baby.
They were wonderfully supportive though and extremely patient with me.
Perhaps this was something they had witnessed before.
Maybe other mothers had behaved in the same way.

After one weeks stay, he was able to come home.

Things seemed unusual and adjusting to having two dependent children wasn't easy.
My eldest was content mostly but displayed a great deal of jealousy.

I found that hard to deal with as I did not want my bond with her to become affected.

I think things were exacerbated because my baby boy just would not settle, he would be awake for the majority of the night and a lot through the day too.
I questioned his poor sleeping and was just assured that it was most likely because he was premature.

I took good care of my baby. I fed him, bathed him, changed him and dressed him.
But I failed to find the same instant connection that I had done with my eldest.
I felt horrible, like a terrible mother.

Depression consumed me and my mood swings became hard for all around me.
I would go from extreme low mood to an extremely irritable state.

A visit from my health visitor recognised my struggles and referred me for some CBT therapy.
I awaited the appointment.

Meanwhile, I continued to take care of my children and the home around them.

My OCD had developed quite significantly during this difficult time.
I was cleaning more and more. Following the same strict routines I had always set myself.
Only, I was doing it through the night also.
I had used it as a tool of distraction. It was a good way to assume some control over my life.
I had spent a lifetime having all decisions taken out of my hands and this was something I could take a hold of.
Something I could decide on and control.

I was like a machine. I survived on as little as two hours sleep each night. Between waking to feed and soothe the baby, I was cleaning and following my strict routine.

I overcame the feelings of tiredness and adapted to life on minimal sleep.

The appointment finally arrived and I dreaded what they would have to say.
I had spent too much time being judged already and I feared them telling me that I was failing. Feared they would want to remove my children from my care.

However it was quite a wait before the appointment so I had no choice but to continue on.

Dad eventually made it round to meet my baby boy. He looked so uneasy holding him.
Mum had already started a new relationship a few months back and both were keen to meet our newest addition.

Mum doted on him as did my sisters and many others.
Dad however did not seem as keen.

Little did I know, this was one of the last moments I would have with my Dad for the next ten years.

I started my course of CBT and opened up about everything occurring in my present life.
It was better than I had anticipated.
I felt ready to tackle some of my demons, ready to put some of my issues to bed.
It wasn't going to be an easy journey, but one I was prepared to take.

NEW OPPORTUNITIES

I was diagnosed with Clinical Depression, Anxiety, OCD, Post-Natal Depression and PTSD.
It was quite a lot to digest.
It wasn't in my nature to give up and so I pushed on and continued to be the best Mum I could be to my two little babies.
They needed me and I was never going to let them down.

I think I was never truly honest with how I was feeling inside and would allow myself to be consumed with emotion. But I would hide it from those around me. I was sure they never noticed.

I was placed on pain medication for my ongoing Arthritic pain and before too long I found myself addicted to what I was taking.
I had discovered that this particular medication provided me with a relaxed sensation and erased all the tension I was constantly walking around with.

Unfortunately though as time went on, my dependency grew.

Before long I was taking double the prescribed dose on the packet.

As my tolerance to the medication increased so did the quantity in which I took it.

Eventually I was taking five times the recommended dose on the packet.

I spent most days using the medication to mask the thoughts and feelings within my body.

It became a struggle to get regular prescriptions from the doctor as they were unaware of my over usage.

So I would ask my Grandad who had an array of pain medication. He would happily oblige and so I then found I was frequently asking him instead.

The habit became unmanageable and I found that I was now struggling to function to the best of my ability and I didn't like the person I was becoming.

It took some strength and courage but I finally admitted to my therapist that I had a problem.

She was unbelievably understanding and sought immediate help for me.

I was referred for drug counselling and immediately placed on a weaning medication.

Unfortunately when I first began taking this medication, I was misinformed with the time scale in which I had to wait to begin.

I overdosed on the combined medications and required an ambulance.

Fortunately no serious harm was caused and I was on the mend very quickly after the incident.

I continued to take the weaning drug prescribed by my doctor and attended my drug counselling sessions.

RAINBOWS

I eventually managed to kick the disgusting habit I had
developed and moved along with my life.

It had been a long year of battles, therapy and fighting my
ever going depression.

With encouragement from my health visitor, I started to
attend toddler groups.
This was a bold move for me and one which sent my
anxiety levels sky high.
But I was so proud of myself for walking through those
doors and quickly was made to feel welcome.

I made a good friend in the lady that managed the group
and good relationships with the other staff members.
This group was my lifesaver and the socialising was just
what I needed.
Before long I was volunteering at the group. I took great
enjoyment out of helping to set up, helping to clear away
and prepping the fruit.
I was offered a permeant volunteer role and I absolutely
loved it.
As the year went on and my work with the group had
increased, they offered me a permanent, paid position.

I was utterly thrilled with my new opportunity and
accepted!

They agreed to send me on a childcare course and a
handful of other training courses.
I was excited to begin my new role and learn new skills.

This would open many doors for me, I could feel it.

A GREAT LOSS

I thrived off all of the new skills I was developing, took
great pride in telling people what I was achieving.
It made me feel good.

Back home, things had improved with my mental health
and I could finally see a light at the end of a very long and
dark tunnel.

As I enjoyed watching my little ones grow, I had noticed
clear differences in their development.
My baby boy was very different to his sister and a lot
slower when learning to do things.
I was aware that children develop at different rates but he
really was having a tough time progressing.
He also seemed to struggle to show emotion and would
often sit and look very complacent.

I flagged up my concerns with the health visitor and she
agreed and referred him to a Paediatrician.

It wasn't long before his difficulties were recognised and he was diagnosed with Autistic Spectrum Disorder. (ASD). This came of no surprise to me and made no difference of course to how much I loved him.
It only made me fight harder and reluctant to give up on ensuring he had the best future.

I was given lots of support over the years for my son and his nursey were wonderfully patient. He had regular appointments at the hospital and I attended groups to educate myself further on his condition.
I found it very useful, it helped me to manage his difficulties at home and build good strategies for helping him to cope.

Meanwhile I continued to pursue my training within the Children's Centre and spent most evenings studying.

I had completed Paediatric First Aid, Safeguarding, Child Protection, Makaton and a course to help run a brand new group with an existing colleague.
I was loving my new developing skills profile.

This is around the time I discovered I was pregnant again.
It was very unexpected and I was concerned the Children's Centre would not want me to pursue my college course.
I couldn't have been more wrong.
They were very supportive and throughout my pregnancy I continued and successfully completed and passed my Diploma in Childcare.
I was unbelievably proud of my achievement.

Shortly after I gave birth to my baby girl via a planned Cesarean Section.
She was wonderful, she was the perfect addition to my little family and her siblings utterly adored her.
In the years I had been working for the Children's Centre,

I had moved home.
I was far more content in my new residence and it was
ideal for my ever growing family.

My Nan was struggling with a diagnosis of Cancer and my
Mum, sisters and I often spent a lot of time by her side.
Between studying and working, I used all my free time in
the care facilities in which she was staying.

I think when she was first diagnosed, I couldn't believe
that it would actually beat her. I failed to see how one of
the strongest women I knew and loved so very much,
could possibly ever leave us.

We spent many nights in the week, uncomfortably
slouched on the chair beside her bed. We would make an
attempt to shut our eyes but it never seemed possible.

As her condition progressed and it was obvious she was
never going to improve, we barely left the care home.
We had a tag team arrangement and would take it in turns
to return home to eat and wash.

I bought my three little ones in to see her several times,
they only ever see their Nan and were too young to see the
weakening lady that we all did.

She held onto my newest addition and smiled from ear to
ear.I treasure this memory dearly.

November 5th 2011, we received the call we had all
dreaded.
She was gone.

BOXING DAY

My depression seemed to have peaked again, I was struggling with an increase in flashbacks and nightmares. My PTSD felt unmanageable and I was having a difficult time, juggling all of my responsibilities.

After saying a final goodbye to my Nan and laying her body to rest, I struggled to adjust to life without her.

Working felt that much harder now and being a single Mum, took its toll.

My Mum was very supportive and we all held each other up. Deep down we knew our family just wouldn't be the same again.

One afternoon I had been called for an unexpected meeting with my manager. I was a little anxious to what it could be about and in true fashion I found myself in a state of panic.

After attending the meeting, it came to light that a previous, routine medical I had to have was the highlight for discussion.
Effectively I was relieved of my duties due to my struggling mental health and asked to move on from the Children's Centre.

This was a hard blow to take and a huge setback for my confidence.
It sent me tumbling straight back to the bottom. Back where I used to be.

I missed my Nan dearly and couldn't imagine my life without her in it.
I lost count of the occasions in which I would pick up the telephone to call her. Only to realise she wasn't there.
My Mum struggled to adjust to life without her in it and it was incredibly sad to see her fall apart.

I spent most days, weeks, even months after her death. Playing her favourite songs on loop. Looking through old photos. Wishing she was still there.
She always knew how to make everything better, always knew how to bring comfort in times of need.

She was one of the strongest women I had ever known. An inspiration to us all. But she was gone and sadly life moves forward and so we had to move along with it.

I successfully retuned to therapy once more and spent months working through the issues I had previously faced. I addressed lots of underlying problems and it helped me to cope with life again.
I dedicated my life to my three small ones. I was the best

RAINBOWS

Mum I could be and everything I did was for them.
I continued to live with an OCD but through lots of
support and therapy had seen it reduce and I was finally
more content with how things were.

I felt stable once more.

Christmas arrived and I did all I could to make sure it was
just perfect for the children. We had a lovely time and I
took great pleasure in seeing the older two rip open their
gifts with great joy in their faces.

Boxing day only bought more sad news though.
My Aunty had passed away.

She was the Aunty I had chosen. She was not biologically
related to any of us but a huge part of our family. She was
my Aunty and always would be.
She was another tough one in character. Someone who
never failed to bring a smile and joy to every room that she
entered.

She showered my children with the same love and
attention as she always had with me.
They too, referred to her as Aunty.

She would be missed dearly by all that knew her.
She was well known within the community and I knew
that so many of those people would be incredibly sad to
see her go.

What an absolutely tragic way to end the year.

THE VOID

I loved my children dearly and they truly made my life a
great pleasure to live but I always felt as if there was
something missing.

A deep loneliness within my heart craved something a little
bit more.

My sister had come over for a visit one day and made
suggestive jokes about me building an online dating
profile.
I laughed and shrugged it off.
With much persuasion though and a roll of my eyes, I
reluctantly agreed to it.

I felt silly almost, trying to write paragraphs on what would
make me desirable.
It wasn't in my nature to find positive things about myself
so building this profile proved tough.
Selecting a photograph proved even harder though as I
hated having my picture taken.

Eventually I settled on a snap of me at a friend's previous house party.
I was just about content with using that one and my online profile was complete.

I closed the laptop and had almost forgotten about the online profile that I had created.
I wasn't optimistic that anyone would show any interest in me.
I wasn't exactly an oil painting to look at and I came with three small packages.
I knew how hard it would be to convince anyone to see past all of that.

My children came first though and anyone not willing to accept them along with me, could just move on by.

My good friend had recently announced her pregnancy to me and I was so over the moon for her and her husband.
She and I were closer than ever and our friendship had blossomed somewhat in the last few years.
We usually see each other once a week and enjoyed spending time offloading our daily struggles to one another.
She had lost her Mum previously and I had tried my best to support her through some very dark and difficult times.
I couldn't imagine the pain she must have been feeling but I tried in whatever way I could, to lift her up and be there when she needed a friend.

My best friend from my youth was still a part of my life too and we had both shared our second pregnancies together.
She was now separated from her partner but was raising two children incredibly well on her own.

I was lucky to have some good friendships.

I had formed an unusual friendship with my youngest
sisters ex-boyfriend and he conveniently lived in the block
of flats situated behind my house.
We seemed an unusual pairing but we had a strong
friendship and he was always there when I needed him.
We would spend many a night, playing on the computer,
discussing our life worries and generally just having a
giggle.
He was a blessing and a friend I was grateful to have.

My life was filled with so many people that cared for me.
So many that supported me and gave me their time.
Yet that void still remained and I still continued to feel as
if something was missing.

One Sunday afternoon, I was busy clearing away after a
roast dinner.
Something I traditionally did every week.

I remembered my online dating profile and decided to give
it a little look.
I opened my laptop and rested it upon the kitchen counter.

Much to my surprise, a message flashed up.
I knew this face, recognised this name.

He was the face I had started my initial shift with at the
cinema. We had become online friends on our social
networking pages and occasionally would speak. But
nothing more than a wishing you well conversation.

He was complementary straight from the off and quite the
charmer.
I was hooked.

We eventually exchanged numbers and spent every day for

a couple of weeks chatting. He was the breath of fresh air I
had been looking for.

CHANGES

I was so nervous on the day that I would finally be
meeting him.
I needn't have been though because we instantly
connected and we felt at ease in each other's company.
It never felt forced, I was content in his arms.
In that moment I realised I never wanted him to leave.

We spent every night for an entire week together and
decided to have one night without seeing each other.
I think in that moment we were concerned that we could
be moving too fast and didn't want to spoil the love that
was growing between us.

That single night felt like a lifetime and we quickly realised
how we couldn't bear to be apart.
Over the weeks, we spent more and more time together.
We went on dates, spent cosy nights in and had days out
with the children
He utterly adored them all and they were besotted with

him especially my youngest.

We made the leap to move in with one another and he
came to join my little family.
He naturally fitted straight in and it was as if he had always
been there, I couldn't remember a time without him in it.

I told him of all my past and shared all my demons. Yet he
remained firmly by my side and supported me through all
my difficulties.

We booked a lovely holiday away together and my Mum
kindly took care of the children whilst we were away.
It was lovely to have that time together. We knew it was a
once in a lifetime trip, whilst the children were still young.
We missed them dreadfully though and could not wait to
get back to them.
Back to the little family we had become.

He always encouraged me to do things for myself. Always
pushed me to do great things and always see the best
within me.
With his encouragement, I applied for a new role within an
nursery and I got the job!

I enjoyed my new role and my colleagues were a lovely
bunch to work alongside.
My life was just how I had imagined. A job I loved, a man
that adored me, my beautiful children and good friends.
For the first time in years, I felt complete.

A telephone call, not much after I had begun my new role,
bought more sad news.
My Mum had called to say that my brothers biological
father had sadly passed away. I know she took the news
hard.
Even though they were no longer an item and she had of

course been an relationship with her new partner for many years, it was still hard news to swallow.
I think a great deal of her sadness related to how it may affect my brother and the impact it could have on his mental health.

It was a sad day saying goodbye and I helped support my Mum through these dark times and was there at the end of the phone, whenever she needed me.

I continued to enjoy my job within the nursey and developed many new skills along the way.
I attended many new courses and eventually trained to become a SENCO. (Special Educational Needs Coordinator).
This was an area of childcare that I felt most passionate about so it was a wonderful opportunity.
I found with my growing knowledge and understanding of specific disabilities, it would help with the strategies and coping mechanisms I would put in place at home for my son.

I was given the opportunity to progress in my career and successfully landed the role of Deputy Manager whilst the current one went off on maternity leave.
It was a great deal of responsibility but I enjoyed it so very much. I enjoyed my job very much but it was becoming tough, juggling the children, home life and getting the children to school was becoming increasingly harder.

Once my youngest had left nursery, issues that were flagged up there, then became more obvious to us at home.
She was struggling to be apart from us both and really wasn't settling into school.
She was having difficulties with a regression in her toilet training and her aggression was becoming more frequent

and harder to manage.

I eventually made the hard but right decision to leave my job.

NEW VENTURES

Other than the births of my children.
The greatest day of my life was upon me.
I was marrying my soul mate, the bestest friend I had ever
had.
It was one of the most nerve racking experiences of my
life but the happiest and most beautiful day I had ever
seen.
I felt as if I were on cloud nine. My puzzle was finally
complete.
He was the missing piece.

Life as a married couple only bought us closer together
and we embraced married life.
I was proud to call him my husband, proud to be his wife.
He see the best in me, always. Made me feel special, loved
and wanted.
He was incredible with the children and together we made

an incredible parenting team.

He would spend hours reading them stories, taking them to the park or building endless creations from Lego.

We were a solid unit, and we faced everything together.

I had always enjoyed baking and this was something I did even more now that I wasn't in full time employment. My husband encouraged me to consider setting up an home run cake baking business.

I had so little confidence and so it took much persuasion before I decided to give it a try.

It was all official, I had registered my business. It was all above board and I completed all the necessary training courses.

It wasn't easy in the beginning and I wasn't as good as some of the well-established cake makers within the community. But I continued to learn and throughout my entire journey, I managed to teach myself new things every day.

Once established, I began taking on orders and it gave me a great sense of pride.

Things were just lovely within our home. Our little family made us so proud. My husband did work some long hours though and so we cherished the time we had together.

In September 2014 we traveled to Nottingham. I was going to undergo some surgery to potentially change our future. Back when I had given birth to my third born, I had been

sterilised. Meaning I could no long carry a child.
However this surgery I was about to have, would change all of that.

After hours of worry from my husband, I was finally awake.
The road to recovery was hard but between my family and friends, I managed to get through and made a full recovery.
The operation was a success and I was told that my chances for conception were good.

It wasn't long before my husband had taken on an additional role alongside his full time job.
He had trained and qualified as an on-call Firefighter.
This obviously took more time away from us as a family, but I supported him greatly and was so proud of what he had achieved.

As a whole, things were wonderful.
My business was beginning to take off, my husband was enjoying his new career and the children seemed happy.

We continued to face daily battles with our third child, the school in which she attended didn't seem to help much either.
We knew that she would face many more struggles as the years passed and would never give up fighting her corner.

Our son was receiving all the help he requited and with the support from us at home, was managing things really well.

The day I had awaited came, two lines on a test.
I could not believe how quickly it had happened, it would seem I was pregnant.

RAINBOWS

But the days following my discovery proved to be
confusing and I was sure that something wasn't quite right.

A RAINBOW

Sure enough, I had been right and what followed bought some unbelieve pain and sadness.

I began bleeding and as I had feared, was miscarrying. The tiny little bean, that had barely began to grown, was now breaking away from me.

It was a trying time and one that evoked so much emotion for myself and my husband.
The few people that I had confided in were very supportive and I couldn't have been more grateful to have them at my side.
However, there were always the occasional one that would pass unhelpful and very hurtful comments.
"Luckily you have children already", "at least you weren't far along".
This was my baby, brushing aside how tiny and undeveloped they were, this was a part of me and a part of the man I loved.

Here we were losing it. Before we had a chance to enjoy
my developing bump, before we had a chance to meet
them and tell them how much we loved them.

It took some time to grieve over the baby we never got to
meet.
We leaned on each other and helped to keep each other
going.
We found ways to cope eventually and found each day a
little easier to deal with, knowing our little bean would
remain in our hearts forever.

Leading up to my reversal I had joined an online support
network for other women in similar situations to I.
I found this to be a good source of comfort and
reassurance though these dark times.
Shortly after my surgery, I was asked to help in the running
of the group.
I happily obliged and knew I had so much support and
words of wisdom to offer many other ladies.
I enjoyed giving back to this community of lost ladies and
it gave me a great deal of joy to help them.

I continued to bake and my business was growing daily. I
was building a great client base and orders were coming in
thick and fast.
It was a great distraction and I thoroughly enjoyed doing it
too.

It wasn't long before I discovered I was pregnant again.
I really struggled to allow myself any happiness this time
though and became extremely paranoid with any twinge,
ache or pain.
I had convinced myself that I would not be meeting this
baby and things would end in exactly the same manner as
they had before.
It made things tough and I refused to purchase anything

for the baby for the majority of my pregnancy.

I took comfort from her movements inside me and loved to feel her kick. Although I periodically checked her beating heart with a home doppler I had purchased and had frequent visits to the hospital and doctors.
I loved this little person growing inside of me and yet I couldn't allow myself to ever believe I would hold her in my arms.

My husband was supportive as ever and held my hand throughout it all.
My Mum and Mother in-law were both extremely supportive too.
I had wonderful relationships with them both and often wondered how I would do things without them.

I spent time confiding in them both, seeking help and support and enjoyed being in their company.
Of course there were my handful of good friends too, but with busy lives and working schedules, it wasn't always easy to make time to see them.

In the last eight weeks of my pregnancy, I reluctantly agreed to begin purchasing the things we needed for her.

I would frequently stand staring at her empty cot and little dresses and still failed to see how I would ever have a little person to fill them.

Soon enough though and earlier than anticipated, I went into labour.
Her due date was not for another few weeks and so I was feeling a little apprehensive.
But after a couple of days in an hospital bed, our baby girl was safely delivered via a Cesarean Section.

MOVES

Adjusting to life with a newborn was tough.
Adjusting to sleepless nights again, long days and the
pressures of ensuring the others had plenty of my time
too.
My husband had arranged so he could have some holiday
time alongside his paternity leave, which was a huge relief
and help for me.
He helped with the school runs, shared the load of the
housework and allowed me to sleep when needed.
I couldn't have asked for any better.

Breastfeeding was taking its toll and I was feeling
incredibly drained with it.
I made the choice to move onto bottles so then I could
share the feeding responsibility.

We adored our new little ray of sunshine and she bought
so much joy into all of our lives.
Her siblings utterly doted on her and enjoyed spending
time giving her cuddles.

I could feel myself sinking again though, a familiar feeling
of sadness was consuming my mind again.
My OCD had become increasingly worse and my mood
was slipping dramatically.

I was able to recognise the familiar feelings though and
paid a visit to my doctors surgery.
They referred me onto the mental health team and I would
then need to await an appointment.

We had a wonderful summer, with our annual summer
holiday and days out with the children.
Our new baby girl was growing so much and was quickly
moving herself around the house now.

In November 2016 we moved house.
This was the greatest move we had made for our family.

We moved to a village outside of where we were living.
The house was bigger, the area was quieter and in general
we welcomed the change.

We were extremely content in our new residence and so
were the children.
They enjoyed their bigger bedrooms, more space in the
garden and the lovely open spaces that surrounded us.

We had successfully gained a place for our son in the
village school, however we were not as successful placing
the girls.
We relied on a great deal of help and support from friends
to transport the girls to their school back where we used to
live.

It was a stressful time and they were struggling.
Our third child was having increasingly harder days and
behaviors were becoming harder and harder to manage.

She was very withdrawn still at school and her aggression
was becoming harder to deal with at home.
We fought extremely hard to get these difficulties
recognised by a doctor and by an educational professional.
So far we were having no joy but this did not stop us
fighting.
It did not deter us from seeking the help she so needed.

Eventually a place was offered to both girls and pressure
had lifted all round.
With all of them in one place, I felt a little more at ease.

I received an appointment to begin my new course of
therapy.
It was something I had never tried before but I was more
than willing to explore new ways to improve my mental
health.
My PTSD was still very much a huge problem and my
depression was at a high once more.
I was diagnosed with having high levels of both and
informed that therapy would be rather intense and
extensive.
This time though, I was prepared for the journey in front
of me.
I was ready to feel better.

EMDR was the name of the therapy I followed with my
therapist.
He was wonderfully patient with me and over the weeks I
began to see a huge improvement.
My nightmares started to decrease and the other symptoms
alongside it seemed to occur less frequently.
It would seem, I had finally found the right type of
support. This was long overdue.

I could see clarity in my mind and a better future with my
mental health.

SADNESS AND JOY

We continued to pursue help for our third child. Her new
school were incredibly supportive and implemented so
many things to help her.
They had recognised her difficulties and were at her side
whilst we pursued the help from outside professionals.

She had great difficulty in separating from me and often
refused to go to school.
Any demand within the day could see her tumbling into a
meltdown.
Particular textures left her distressed and she could not
cope in loud and busy environments.
I think it had soon become obvious, that like her brother,
she too was on the Autistic Spectrum.

This year had seen so many changes and my Mum was
struggling after being diagnosed with Bowel Cancer.
I would never have admitted to her just how scared we all
were during this time.
How we paced up and down whilst she underwent major
surgery to remove her bladder.
How we secretly prayed she would not be taken

prematurely from this world.
We all watched her crumble when she adjusted to a head
of no hair. Helped make her smile when the
Chemotherapy made her extremely sick.

She was tough beyond belief though and we all knew she
had the ability to fight this, even if she didn't feel that way
herself.

I continued with my therapy and felt better and better
within myself every day. I was now running the online
support group that I had been a part of for so long.
I felt honoured to have had it handed over to me.

My husband had changed careers and was now enjoying
life as a Postman. This allowed us more time together and
he was able to enjoy more time with the children.

One morning as he set off to work, a familiar feeling
stirred within my stomach.
My period had been absent and I was unexpectedly late.
I waited for him to leave before taking that familiar test.

I patiently plodded on throughout the house. Completing
my usual morning routine.
I then lifted the test, although I think if I was truly honest,
I was already sure of the result.
It was of course, positive.

I dialed my Husband and told him the news over the
telephone.
He didn't seem surprised but I could hear the happiness in
his voice.
Another baby would be bought into our loving home and
this time I felt more able to enjoy the wonderful news.
Better stability with my mental health, really helped with
this.

A NEW ARRIVAL

With the happy news that my Mums Cancer was clear and
each checkup revealed how well she was recovering, things
were looking brighter than ever.

We had more involvement form outside agencies and
professionals and a better network of support for our third
born.

It was hard to see her fall apart daily. Hard to see the
rollercoaster of emotions that she experienced.
From a meltdown, to aggressive behaviors, to screaming.
Followed by sobbing and exhaustion.
It was hard for all involved.

She would frequently target her siblings and lash out at us
too.
She was placed on the SEN register at school and
provided with limited 1:1 support.
This proved helpful for her and we appreciated it.

Before long we welcomed our baby boy into the world.
He was absolutely beautiful and I could not wait to take
him home to join our family.

Just as I had expected, they all loved him very much.
They had so much time for him and it soon felt as if he
had been a part of our family forever.

We took great joy in watching him grow and develop and
his siblings took pleasure in teaching him new things every
day.

As the summer loomed, we went for a visit at an specialist
Autistic school.
We had intended on transferring our eldest son there.
It was what was in his best interests and the right move for
his future.
After a successful visit, we made an application for an in-
year school transfer.

We enjoyed time together as a large and loud family and
took frequent days out.
After another, lovely family holiday, we attended the
wedding of my sister and new brother in law.

It was a beautiful service and I was thrilled she had found
someone to make a life and future with.

My therapy came to a close and I was no longer deemed at
risk. Was no longer viewed at a dangerous level.
I finally felt free from the demons that had consumed me
for so many years.
Free from all the pain I had endured for the majority of
my life.
I knew to expect the occasional slip up, I knew that all
would not be entirely perfect.
But I was finally content with my mental state.

I finally felt more able to deal with whatever life could throw at me now.

We see a huge increase in the difficult behaviors and challenges from our third born and I think we admittedly were having a really tough time handling it all.

I took great comfort in confiding in a good friend who knew of my struggles and felt them on a more personal level.
She too had children on the spectrum. One of which appeared to have similar difficulties to our daughter.
It was a great comfort knowing we were not alone.
We would often meet to chat and share our troubles and tribulations.

We would also confide our inner struggles and share strategies with each other.
She was a huge asset and a friend I had grown to hugely adore. She was a good support for me and helped to bring clarity on days where I couldn't see clear enough.
I will forever be grateful for the friend I have in her.

With no joy yet with our eldest sons in-year school application, we were beginning to worry what his future may hold and the difficulties we would all face together.

We had made the decision to have no more children and to focus on and enjoy the beautiful family we had already.
After making that very final decision we had some very difficult and emotional moments.
A undeniable strain had been placed upon our marriage, but once more we stood tall together throughout.
I know how my husband struggled and I was also aware of how he felt too proud to admit.
I am so proud of him for facing his demons though and

seeking support.
He should be seen as an inspiration to many men and
hopefully encouragement to others on the importance of
speaking up.

MEMORY MAKING

As we began a new year, we vowed that would spend it building more memories, trying new things and spending more time together as a family.

My husband had had a career change and was now content within his new role.
He was doing something he had longed to do which involved him giving back something to the community.
The support he gave within his role was incredibly challenging but most certainly very rewarding.
He was now settled in his position and seemed happier leaving for work every day.

His new role meant he didn't have to work throughout the school holidays.
It had been lovely having him home for Christmas and we were looking forward to sharing each of the school holidays with him.
In his spare time he still enjoyed exercise and his passion

lay with boxing.
He trained regularly and it proved to be a great healer and
aid to his new positive frame of mind.
He had competed in a few different competitions and I
had been there by his side to cheer him on.
He relied on the support I gave him and would often need
a little push of motivation from me to keep him focused.
He appreciated the nudge and continued to pursue and
enjoy the boxing.

In January we celebrated our youngest daughters birthdays
and as always enjoyed the family time we had and more
importantly the cake!
We had kick started our new year really well and finished
the month with a birthday trip, just myself and my
husband. We had the pleasure of feeding some beautiful
tigers.
It was a wonderful experience and another incredible thing
to tick off our bucket list.

Over the next couple of months, we celebrated two more
of our children's birthdays and enjoyed an evening out to
see one of my childhood favourites.
My husband had treated me to an Shakin' Stevens concert.
It was a lovely evening and I was over the moon.
In these few months, the children experienced their first
live football match and our eldest son won his first
competition at school.
This was a huge accomplishment for him.
His lack of confidence had always prevented him from
entering such things, so we were unbelievably proud of
him.

We enjoyed plenty of picnics with close friends, enjoyed
evenings out together and took the children to some lovely
places.
We were so blessed to be able to enjoy all of these things

and I was so grateful for every moment.

My business was thriving more than ever. I was so proud of how far I had come over the years. I had learned a great deal and taught myself so many new skills.
My cake profile was increasing and I had extended the services I offered.
I now provided party buffets, made personalised gifts, made sweet cones, cookies, cupcakes and of course the birthday cakes.
I was regularly booked for public events and sourced by many.
I never believed I could achieve all that I had.

We were invited along to our eldest daughters parents evening. Both of us were proud as punch to discover just how well she was doing.
She was achieving at an unbelievably high level and the teachers had moved her onto work far above her expected age.
Grades most certainly are not what life is about and I would never push mine to stress about them unnecessarily.
But when you have a child that has such a thirst for learning and that takes great pleasure in achieving high, than its hard not to be incredibly proud.

I am forever proud of all of my children and all they have done.
They are all very different but all remarkable in their own ways.

A SAD GOODBYE

My Mum had come over to take care of the children whilst
I attended an hospital appointment after school on day.
My husband would meet me at the hospital to collect me
afterwards.

Whilst at the hospital, I received a telephone phone call
from my Mother in-law.
My Father in-law was in hospital.
They were no longer an item but she still cared a great deal
for him so was feeling concerned for his well-being.

I contacted my husband to make him aware and he
requested for me to pop in and see him whilst I was there.
Of course I happily did so, once I had managed to locate
him.

At his bedside sat his new partner. This was the first time I had met her. She was sat clutching his hand and shared the same concerns my Mother in-law had previously expressed to me.

He did look rather poorly but remained in good spirits.
He was very chatty and we even had a giggle about a few things.
I told him some stories around the children, discussed how my husband's boxing was going and in general had a nice little catch up. It was a shame it was under such circumstances.

My husband arrived at the hospital to collect me and I suggested he pop into the hospital to see his Dad.
He parked up the car and took my place by his bed. I remained in the car with our eldest daughter.

It was a short while before he arrived back at the car and we headed off back home.

The traffic was horrendous and gave us the opportunity to chat about his Dad and for my husband to express his worry around his health.
He intended to return to visit him should he still be in the hospital the following day.

That evening, the telephone rang.
My Father in-law had taken a turn for the worse.
His heart was struggling from what I could understand.

My husband went to the hospital and returned a couple of hours later.
My Father in-law had sadly passed away.

RAINBOWS

My husband appeared quiet and looked to be in a state of
shock. He struggled to get the words to leave his lips.
I spent the night awake, whilst I held my husband close to
me. He spoke briefly about his Dad and I remained at his
side, whilst he shut his eyes for a little while.

The morning seemed so strange. We continued as normal
to get the children ready for school and dropped them off
before heading to my Mother in-laws.

She was understandably in a state of distress and shock
and there was a small gathering of other family members
in her living room.
Lots of tears were shed, plenty of hugs were given and
stories were shared.
I think for all involved it all seemed a little unbelievable
still.

The days that followed were no easier either and my
husband struggled to come to terms with his loss.

I supported him throughout and helped him with all the
funeral preparations.

My husband returned to work and life continued as it
always did.
I could see the clear sadness in my husband's eyes and I
could see how he longed to go back in time.
I could feel the tension and hear the distress in his voice.
I know how he had so many things he still wished to say,
so many things he still wanted to do.
With that time now stolen from him, I knew he would
have a tough time moving forward.

A BLAST FROM THE PAST

One evening in June, my husband and I sat watching the television. Not unusual for a Saturday night.
We often spent time watching the usual rubbish on the box.
This particular night though, we were awake longer than usual, chatting and reminiscing over times gone by.

My phone bleeped whilst we were talking. Again this wasn't out of the ordinary and often I would just ignore it and pick up the message much later.
But on this occasion I opened it up to see who was messaging.

It was a message from my Dad.

He hadn't been in touch for over ten years. This was a huge shock for me and I glared at the phone shaking for quite some time.
Unsure with what to respond with, or whether I wanted to

respond at all, I continued to hold it in disbelief.

He had clearly been drinking based on his illiterate and jumbled words.
He had declared how sorry he was for not contacting me sooner. He expressed his deep sadness for being apart from me and my sisters and how much he longed to have it all back.

I really did not know how to handle it. I had so much I wanted to say. I wanted to yell at him. Wanted to tell him how angry and let down I felt.

With a little nudge from my husband, I replied to his message.

I explained how he had made us all feel, I never held back when explaining how abandoned we all felt.

After the loss of my Father in-law, I felt I needed to give him another chance. I did miss my Dad dearly and wished for one more go at a relationship with him.

I knew my Mum would be upset and I was concerned about telling her along with my sisters.

After much upset from all, they all stood by my decision and my want to give him another opportunity to make a mends.

I think he was truly grateful for being given another chance to make things right and he continued to message me daily.
He was interested to know how the children were doing, asked questions about all the things he had missed and expressed sadness for all the lovely memories he had missed out on making.

Letting my Dad back into my life was a huge decision and one I still remained unsure of.
I still remained cautious and prepared for him to let me down again.
He was keen to meet for a coffee, I however decided I would feel more at ease if I kept him at arm's length.
I think this was mostly due to fearing the rejection again, fearing he would walk out once more.
I did not want to feel that hurt again.

My Father in-laws funeral was fast approaching and we were all just making sure all the last arrangements were in place.
I helped my husband by writing a nice poem to share and organised for flowers to be gifted from us all.

The day was understandably filled with an immense amount of sadness. All of the family had come together and everyone held one another up.

Friends and family continued to share stories of times they had spent with him. People could be seen to be smiling as they shared happy times gone by.

The day was incredibly long and went late on into the evening.
My husband was reacquainted with old faces which bought him some comfort.
We were overwhelmed with how much support and love was given from all.

The funeral left my husband a little shaken again but I do believe helped to bring him some form of closure.
Now he could focus on moving forward and concentrate on mending his broken heart.

PROUD MOMENTS

For the first time in a while, my husband and I enjoyed an
evening at the races and a Kaiser Chiefs concert.
He had previously won a competition so it wasn't
something we had planned.
All the same, it was lovely to be out and we both enjoyed
our first experience at the races and the concert was
amazing.

The prep work had begun for my Mum and Step-Dads
wedding.
The nerves were building and we were all trying to help
out where we could.
I created some beautiful gifts for them both, wrote a poem
and of course the cake was my responsibility.
After an extremely stressful morning, I had finally
completed the cake. I was actually incredibly proud of the

finished product and knew that they would both love it.

The wedding was just perfect and Mum looked absolutely beautiful.
They both looked so happy as they exchanged vows and the service was just lovely.
They had a gathering at their home, with buffet food, drinks and decorations.
It was nice to see family and friends that we had not seen for some time.
It was nice to catch up.

However two of the children were struggling in the busy and extremely crowded environment. So we left sooner than we had anticipated.

They thoroughly enjoyed their day though and I was thrilled for them finally coming together as husband and wife.

The next month, we headed off to Butlins for the first time ever.
We had the most incredible time and spent so much time together as a family.
My Mother in-law always went away with us. It truly would not be the same without her there. The children enjoyed her coming along and so did we.
We filled our time with so many delightful things.
We visited the circus, the cinema, played golf and bowling too.
Had a blast at the fairground, went swimming and spent time in the soft play.
We ate in some lovely places and see some wonderful shows.
We were lucky enough to see and meet Stephen Mulhern, watched Diversity perform and got to meet Paddington Bear!

We made a huge amount of memories and were sad to leave it all behind.

When we returned home, our third child made a choice to have her hair chopped off.
Her hair was extremely long and she had many sensory issues surrounding her head and the touch on her hair.
I was a little apprehensive on how it may go, but I supported her decision.
She then made the choice to donate her golden locks to a wig building charity.
These wigs are developed for children experiencing hair loss, due to illnesses such as Cancer.
She made us so proud.

Over the last few months, leading up to her hair donation.
She had been on a complete mission to clean up our village.
It saddened her, that others could be so selfish and drop their rubbish onto the floor.
With my help, she would collect rubbish every day after school.
She was so selfless and always looking at ways to help other people.

My eldest sons in-year school transfer would soon need to be replaced by an brand new application and so I then had begun a brand new application.
This was a phase transfer request.
It was to ensure he didn't attend a mainstream secondary school.
His new application was submitted and all we could do now was hope.

WINNER

My husband had been training hard for an upcoming fight. He was boxing to win a title and would be awarded with a belt, should he win.
He trained more regularly than usual and put a great deal of time into ensuring he was at his fittest for it.
He amended his diet and took every opportunity he could get to work out.

As the night approached, he become increasingly nervous and even suggested that he didn't do it.

I assured him that I would be at his side like always and in the crowd cheering him on.

I admittedly sat fairly anxious, on the edge of my seat as I waited for it to be his turn in the ring.
He had worked so hard and I knew how much it meant to him.

It was finally his turn, out he walked to his chosen music track and climbed into the ring.

Being a title fight, it went on longer than the usual fight.
Much more than he been used to.
He seemed to be doing so well and I continued to cheer
him on.
Win or lose, I was always proud of him for having the
courage to be there in the first place.
Results time and I sat twiddling my thumbs as the referee
stood central to both boxers.

They lifted my husband's arm and pronounced him the
winner!
I couldn't quite believe it and by the look on his face,
neither could he.
I was so completely proud of him.
His hard work and determination had paid off.
He proudly held up his belt and didn't part with it for the
remainder of the evening.

My husband intended to retire on this win and informed
me that he would not competitively box any more.
Although I'm not sure I believed him.
It wasn't the first time he had said that.

Our youngest daughter was starting nursery and it brought
happy and sad tears to us both.
I always felt sad on these occasions but I knew she was
ready for this next phase in her life.
She looked so grown up in her uniform and excited to
make new friends.
She went in a bit wobbly at first and after a couple of
mornings of tears, she eventually settled and looked
forward to going.
She was growing in confidence and it was lovely to see.

We celebrated our eldest sons birthday and our anniversary

and another month had flown by.

As we entered October, we see the end of our eldest
daughters Masterclasses.
She had been attending them for the last six weeks.
This was something they held for high performing children
within school.
They are given the opportunity to attend these Saturday
classes for a short period of time.
The aim is to learn things they would not ordinarily be
learning at this age at school and so to give them a better
insight into things.
This particular course was to cover Math's and held in
Cambridge.
She did incredibly well, as expected and we attended her
last session to see her awarded with a certificate of
completion.
Another proud parent moment.

My husband and I were given the opportunity for another
evening out.
We were greatly enjoying all the memory making we had
done this year and all the extra time we had allowed
ourselves as a couple.
On this occasion we were heading out for an evening with
Frank Bruno.
It was a fabulous evening filled with lots of laughter.
My husband was thrilled at being given the opportunity to
chat to Frank and managed to meet him briefly at the end
of the show.

We looked forward to planning more moments just like
this.

BATTLES

New battles commenced this month and the next few
months would prove to be rather stressful indeed.
We had made an application for an EHCP (Educational
Health and Care Plan) for our daughter and she had finally
been accepted for an appointment with the community
Paediatrician.
The school were still incredible with their support and had
introduced more things in order to make her day a little bit
more bearable.

She had prompt cards to help with her communication
and sensory breaks during the day.
A relaxed approach to her learning was implemented and
she started her school day earlier than her peers.

We continued to build evidence and compile things in
order to get her the long term support she so deserved.

I submitted all the relevant paperwork and the rest was now a waiting game.
We were still awaiting some communication from my sons potential new school.
We were beginning to feel rather deflated at the lack of progress we had made in what was over a year now.
My son still had no assigned school placement for his secondary years and we were becoming increasingly frustrated with it all.

I received some wonderful news via email though.
Our daughter had been nominated for a Community Inspiration Award for her work with rubbish collecting.
We were so thrilled for her and beamed with pride.
She won the award at the ceremony and was later sent a beautiful award that now sits proudly upon a shelf in our living room.
She was over the moon with her shiny trophy and the gifts that she received along with it.

We received the bad news that the EHCP application was refused and that I would then have to make an appeal.
I had to compile even more evidence and fill in even more paperwork.
I attended umpteen more meetings and kick started the process for an appeal.

I tried to switch off during the Christmas period. I wanted to ignore all the paperwork, forget the meetings and focus on my family for the next three weeks.

We had the most enjoyable Christmas time and had fun creating some brand new traditions.

I now felt ready and raring as we edged into 2020.

PROGRESS

We started the new year with our daughter Paediatrician appointment.
She was highly anxious and struggled to complete all of the things being asked of her.
The appointment lasted for an hour or so and she was left feeling quite down afterwards.
As it was her birthday and she had been authorised the entire day off school, I happily treated her to a delicious lunch.
It really helped to pick her up and she quickly forgot about the stress from the appointment.

She received a referral to the team at the hospital to help with her bedtime issues, a referral for Occupational Therapy team and one for the clinical Phycologist.
It finally felt as if we were making some good progress.

A letter from the Paediatrician listed all of her difficulties
and gave a diagnosis.
It was what we had waited for, for so long.
We finally had clarity and a way moving forward.
She would finally get the long awaited help she needed.

We are still awaiting progress on our appeal but are
content with what is currently in place for her.
We still battle daily and still struggle at times.
But with better strategies in place we feel more able to
help her get through the tough moments and help her to
cope in situations that she feels particularly taxing.,

Almost two years on since our initial expression of interest
in a particular school for our son and we have failed in our
attempt to get him in.
We are now exploring other options but continue to fight
his cause and do not intend on giving up till he has in place
what is best for him.

Our eldest daughter is soon to make her choices in moving
forward for her GCSE's and we are utterly thrilled with the
progress she has shown through her time there already.

Our youngest daughter continues to love nursery and has
recently overcome her fear of the toilet.

Our youngest son is developing new sentences and skills
every day.

All five of our beautiful children make us proud beyond
belief every day.

MOVING FORWARD

We have had such a positive start to the year and have already enjoyed making some terrific memories.

We enjoyed feeding some giraffes, climbing on top of the O2 in London, cinema trips and more.

At the start of the year I set up a group to build hampers to gift to people in need within the community.
I then joined forces with another group to put together food parcels for people struggling within the community.
We have had such a successful start and have already gifted so many food parcels, toiletries, clothes, toys, books and more.

Over the last month though I did receive a scare that has left me still in a state of worry.

I had tests that revealed levels of Ovarian Cancer in my blood.
I have had to undergo a series of other tests and examinations and now await the results of the final blood test.
The scan results seemed positive so now I keep everything crossed that the remaining bloods will too bring me some good news.

If it is something to face than it's a battle I am prepared for.
I have faced so much in my life, and with better mental stability feel I could battle this too.

It had taken many years to finally build the courage to write this account of my life story and it truly has helped in the healing process.

I am loved by so many and am so fortunate to have so many beautiful souls in my life.

I have a successful business, a thriving online support group and co-run a community based support groups.

I have a beautiful home, incredible children and a husband whom I adore.

I have been free of cigarettes for almost seven years now and only consume small amounts of alcohol on special occasions.

I continue to struggle with my Arthritis but I am hoping that one day, I will too be free from that pain.

I hope in reading this I can help others to see that no

matter what battles you may have to face, no matter what things you may have to endure, it does not have to define you.

In times of sadness and dark moments that see you wanting to give up, know that there is someone always there to offer support.
There is always a service available to help lift you from that hole.
So even on dark and stormy days, remember, there is always the possibility of a rainbow.

RAINBOWS

Printed by Amazon Italia Logistica S.r.l.
Torrazza Piemonte (TO), Italy

13776667R00073